This book belongs to:

*To my daughter, Grace, who is a
continual reminder to me of God's
grace and tender mercies.*

Hello, friend! I'm so happy to have you here! This journal was created during a personal desert—a particularly difficult time that challenged me deeply. However, consider the desert for a moment. It's not simply a vast expanse of sand and scorching sun, but rather a place where life, against all odds, finds a way to bloom. Similar to the cactus growing in an arid wilderness, so too our souls have seasons of drought. It is during these times that our thirst for God becomes evident, our need for His living water most acute.

Whether this season of your life feels like a fruitful, lush garden or you too are walking through a desert, feeling the seer of unanswered questions and the thirst for deeper truths, I invite you to join me in an exploration of scripture and a greater knowledge of who He is.

It is my hope that the simple structure of this journal, with weekly scriptures, thought moments, and spaces for reflection, helps us both as we seek a more profound prayer life. Together, let's walk towards a deeper relationship with God, discovering His truths and promises, just as the cactus discovers hidden waters deep beneath the surface of the sand.

May this journal serve as a tool in your daily devotion, a place where you can pour out your heart and be filled with the encouragement, replenishment, and fulfillment that comes from God's word and a personal relationship with Him.

Your friend & wilderness companion,

About your Journal

This prayer journal is divided into two main parts: a prayer log at the beginning of the book, followed by weekly scriptures, thought moments and guided prayer journaling sections.

The structure of the journal is intended to support a robust prayer time, whether you have five minutes or fifty. Remember, this is YOUR journal, so feel free to be creative and use the sections in whatever way serves your prayer time best.

A Prayer Log is located at the front of your journal for easy access and to act as a continual reminder to document and track answered prayers.

There is space to write out your request, the date prayer began, and the date the prayer is answered.

Scripture & Thought Moment – Each week starts off with a passage of scripture and a "thought moment" quote or author commentary.

These are intended to support your meditation on the Word, uncover Biblical truths, and assist in your intercession time with the Lord.

About your Journal

Biblical Truths – Consider the scripture passage and thought moment on the previous page and write out the biblical truths they bring to light.

Reflection – This is an open-ended section to write out your thoughts and feelings about the scripture and its application in your life and personal circumstances.

On my heart – Capture anything that is weighing on your heart this week.

Gratitude – This section is dedicated to practicing gratitude and thankfulness for all He does for us.

Confession – It's important to acknowledge and seek forgiveness for our mistakes, which is the focus of this section.

Who He is – What is the Lord revealing to you about Himself this week?

Prayer – This section is dedicated to all of your specific prayer requests for the week.

Praise – The Bible tells us in Psalm 100 to enter His gates with thanksgiving and His courts with praise. Capture your praise here!

Digging Deeper
INTO
Scripture

To assist your personal devotion time and desire to delve deeper into God's word, I created a free digital bonus that includes **150** scripture references organized by topic.

Scan the QR code to
get a copy sent
directly to your inbox!

Prayer Log

Prayer Request	Date Started	Date Answered

Prayer Log

Prayer Request	Date Started	Date Answered

Prayer Log

Prayer Request	Date Started	Date Answered

Prayer Log

Prayer Request	Date Started	Date Answered

Prayer Log

Prayer Request	Date Started	Date Answered

Prayer Log

Prayer Request	Date Started	Date Answered

ASK, AND IT WILL BE GIVEN

Ask, and it will be given to you; seek, and you will find; knock, and it will be opened to you.
For everyone who asks receives, and the one who seeks finds, and to the one who knocks it will be opened.

Or what person is there among you who, when his son asks for a loaf of bread, will give him a stone? Or if he asks for a fish, he will not give him a snake, will he?

So if you, despite being evil, know how to give good gifts to your children, how much more will your Father who is in heaven give good things to those who ask Him!

Matthew 7:7-11 NASB

Thought Moment

"Gratitude goes to work informing your faith, reminding you that you have every reason to trust God for the future."

Joni Eareckson Tada

Biblical Truths

_____

_____

_____

_____

_____

_____

_____

Reflection

_____

_____

_____

_____

_____

_____

_____

_____

_____

_____

_____

_____

_____

_____

On my heart 💗

_____
_____
_____
_____
_____
_____
_____
_____
_____
_____
_____
_____
_____
_____
_____
_____
_____
_____

Gratitude

_____
_____
_____
_____
_____
_____
_____
_____
_____
_____
_____
_____
_____
_____
_____

Confession

_____
_____
_____
_____
_____
_____
_____
_____
_____
_____
_____

Who He is _____

_____

Prayer

_____
_____
_____
_____
_____
_____
_____
_____
_____
_____

Praise

_____
_____
_____
_____
_____
_____
_____
_____

HIS PEACE IS A GUARDIAN

Do not be anxious about anything,
but in every situation, by prayer and petition,
with thanksgiving, present your requests to God.
And the peace of God
which transcends all understanding
will guard your hearts and your minds in Christ Jesus.

Philippians 4:6-7 NIV

Thought Moment

"Worrying is carrying tomorrow's load with today's strength – carrying two days at once. It is moving into tomorrow ahead of time. Worrying does not empty tomorrow of its sorrow; it empties today of its strength."

Corrie ten Boom

Biblical Truths _____

_____
_____
_____
_____
_____
_____
_____

Reflection _____

_____
_____
_____
_____
_____
_____
_____
_____
_____
_____
_____
_____
_____
_____

On my heart ♥

_____
_____
_____
_____
_____
_____
_____
_____
_____
_____
_____
_____
_____
_____
_____
_____

Gratitude

_____
_____
_____
_____
_____
_____
_____
_____
_____
_____
_____

Confession

_____
_____
_____
_____
_____
_____
_____
_____
_____

Who He is

Prayer

Praise

THE POWER OF SILENCE

The one who has knowledge uses words with restraint, and whoever has understanding is even-tempered.

Proverbs 17:27 NIV

Thought Moment

"Silence, as someone has said, is the mother of prayer and the nurse of holy thoughts. Silence cuts down on our sins, doesn't it? We can't be sinning in so many different ways if we are being quiet before God. Silence nourishes patience, charity, discretion."

Elisabeth Elliot

Week: _____

Biblical Truths

_____

_____
_____
_____
_____
_____
_____
_____

Reflection

_____

_____
_____
_____
_____
_____
_____
_____
_____
_____
_____
_____
_____
_____
_____
_____

On my heart 🖤

_____
_____
_____
_____
_____
_____
_____
_____
_____
_____
_____
_____
_____
_____
_____
_____
_____
_____

Gratitude

_____
_____
_____
_____
_____
_____
_____
_____
_____
_____

Confession

_____
_____
_____
_____
_____
_____
_____
_____
_____
_____
_____
_____

Who He is _____
_____

Prayer

_____
_____
_____
_____
_____
_____
_____
_____

Praise

_____
_____
_____
_____
_____
_____
_____
_____

THE GOD OF 'RIGHT NOW'

Come to me, all you who are weary and burdened,
and I will give you rest.
Take my yoke upon you and learn from me,
for I am gentle and humble in heart, and you will find
rest for your souls.
For my yoke is easy and my burden is light.

Matthew 11:28-30 NIV

Thought Moment

"God is the God of 'right now.' He doesn't want you sitting around regretting yesterday. Nor does He want you wringing your hands and worrying about the future. He wants you focusing on what He is saying to you and putting in front of you...right now."

Priscilla Shirer, <u>Discerning the Voice of God</u>

Week: _____

Biblical Truths _____

_____
_____
_____
_____
_____
_____
_____

Reflection _____

_____
_____
_____
_____
_____
_____
_____
_____
_____
_____
_____
_____
_____
_____

On my heart ♥

_____
_____
_____
_____
_____
_____
_____
_____
_____
_____
_____
_____
_____
_____
_____
_____
_____
_____
_____

Gratitude

_____
_____
_____
_____
_____
_____
_____
_____
_____
_____
_____
_____

Confession

_____
_____
_____
_____
_____
_____
_____
_____
_____
_____

Who He is _____

Prayer

_____

_____

_____

_____

_____

_____

_____

_____

_____

_____

Praise

_____

_____

_____

_____

_____

_____

_____

_____

_____

HE CALLS FORTH OUR DESTINY

But because of his great love for us, God, who is rich in mercy, made us alive with Christ even when we were dead in transgressions—it is by grace you have been saved. And God raised us up with Christ and seated us with him in the heavenly realms in Christ Jesus, in order that in the coming ages he might show the incomparable riches of his grace, expressed in his kindness to us in Christ Jesus. For it is by grace you have been saved, through faith—and this is not from yourselves, it is the gift of God—not by works, so that no one can boast.

Ephesians 2:4-9 NIV

Thought Moment

"God speaks to who we are becoming, not to who we've been. He calls forth destiny rather than echo history."

Lisa Bevere

Biblical Truths _____

_____
_____
_____
_____
_____
_____
_____
_____

Reflection _____

_____
_____
_____
_____
_____
_____
_____
_____
_____
_____
_____
_____
_____
_____
_____
_____
_____
_____

On my heart 🖤

Gratitude

Confession

Who He is _____

Prayer

_____
_____
_____
_____
_____
_____
_____
_____

Praise

_____
_____
_____
_____
_____
_____
_____

POWER OVER THE STORM

Be alert and of sober mind. Your enemy the devil prowls around like a roaring lion looking for someone to devour. Resist him, standing firm in the faith, because you know that the family of believers throughout the world is undergoing the same kind of sufferings.

And the God of all grace, who called you to his eternal glory in Christ, after you have suffered a little while, will himself restore you and make you strong, firm and steadfast. To him be the power for ever and ever. Amen.

I Peter 5:8-10 NIV

Thought Moment

"God doesn't author hardship but uses it to strengthen us for greater conquests. He never leads us into a storm that He doesn't give us the power to overcome."

John Bevere

Week: _____

Biblical Truths _____

_____
_____
_____
_____
_____
_____
_____

Reflection _____

_____
_____
_____
_____
_____
_____
_____
_____
_____
_____
_____
_____
_____
_____

On my heart ♥

_____
_____
_____
_____
_____
_____
_____
_____
_____
_____
_____
_____
_____
_____
_____
_____
_____

Gratitude

_____
_____
_____
_____
_____
_____
_____
_____
_____
_____
_____

Confession

_____
_____
_____
_____
_____
_____
_____
_____
_____
_____

Who He is _____
_____

Prayer

_____
_____
_____
_____
_____
_____
_____
_____
_____

Praise

_____
_____
_____
_____
_____
_____
_____

MEDITATE ON HIM

On the glorious splendor of Your majesty
and on Your wonderful works, I will meditate.

Psalm 145:5 NASB

"An unschooled man who knows how to meditate upon the Lord has learned far more than the man with the highest education who does not know how to meditate."

Charles Stanley

Week: _____

Biblical Truths _____

_____
_____
_____
_____
_____
_____
_____
_____

Reflection _____

_____
_____
_____
_____
_____
_____
_____
_____
_____
_____
_____
_____
_____
_____
_____
_____

On my heart 🖤

_____
_____
_____
_____
_____
_____
_____
_____
_____
_____
_____
_____
_____
_____
_____
_____
_____

Gratitude

_____
_____
_____
_____
_____
_____
_____
_____
_____
_____
_____
_____

Confession

_____
_____
_____
_____
_____
_____
_____
_____
_____
_____
_____

Who He is

Prayer

Praise

PEACE IN DIFFICULTY

The Lord also keeps safe those who suffer.
He is a safe place in times of trouble.
Those who know Your name will put their trust
in You. For You, O Lord, have never left alone
those who look for You.

Psalm 9:9-10 NLV

Thought Moment

"Life with God is not immunity from difficulties, but peace in difficulties."

C. S. Lewis

Biblical Truths _____

_____
_____
_____
_____
_____
_____
_____
_____

Reflection _____

_____
_____
_____
_____
_____
_____
_____
_____
_____
_____
_____
_____
_____
_____
_____
_____

On my heart ♥

Gratitude

Confession

Who He is _____
_____

Prayer

_____
_____
_____
_____
_____
_____
_____
_____
_____
_____

Praise

_____
_____
_____
_____
_____
_____
_____
_____

LIVING WITH A GRATEFUL HEART

The Lord is my shepherd, I lack nothing.
He makes me lie down in green pastures,
he leads me beside quiet waters, he refreshes my soul.
He guides me along the right paths for his name's sake.
Even though I walk through the darkest valley,
I will fear no evil for you are with me;
your rod and your staff, they comfort me.
You prepare a table before me in the presence of my enemies.
You anoint my head with oil; my cup overflows.
Surely your goodness and love will follow me
all the days of my life,
and I will dwell in the house of the Lord forever.

Psalm 23:1-6 NIV

Thought Moment

"The more you live with a grateful heart, praising God for what
He's done and thanking Him for all He's given you, the more you
will see His goodness and then release it into and through your life."

Robert Morris

Biblical Truths _____

_____
_____
_____
_____
_____
_____
_____
_____

Reflection _____

_____
_____
_____
_____
_____
_____
_____
_____
_____
_____
_____
_____
_____
_____

On my heart ♥

_____
_____
_____
_____
_____
_____
_____
_____
_____
_____
_____
_____
_____
_____
_____
_____
_____
_____

Gratitude

_____
_____
_____
_____
_____
_____
_____
_____
_____
_____
_____
_____

Confession

_____
_____
_____
_____
_____
_____
_____
_____
_____
_____
_____

Who He is _____
_____

Prayer

_____
_____
_____
_____
_____
_____
_____
_____

Praise

_____
_____
_____
_____
_____
_____
_____

GROWING MORE LIKE CHRIST

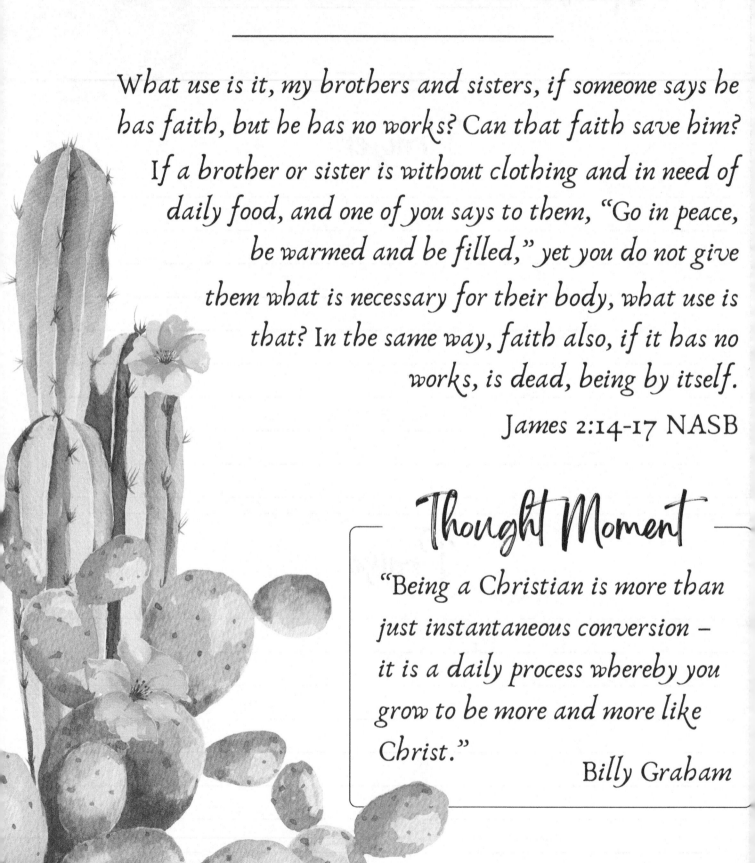

What use is it, my brothers and sisters, if someone says he has faith, but he has no works? Can that faith save him? If a brother or sister is without clothing and in need of daily food, and one of you says to them, "Go in peace, be warmed and be filled," yet you do not give them what is necessary for their body, what use is that? In the same way, faith also, if it has no works, is dead, being by itself.

James 2:14-17 NASB

Thought Moment

"Being a Christian is more than just instantaneous conversion – it is a daily process whereby you grow to be more and more like Christ."

Billy Graham

Biblical Truths _____

_____
_____
_____
_____
_____
_____
_____

Reflection _____

_____
_____
_____
_____
_____
_____
_____
_____
_____
_____
_____
_____
_____
_____
_____

On my heart ♥

_____
_____
_____
_____
_____
_____
_____
_____
_____
_____
_____
_____
_____
_____
_____
_____

Gratitude

_____
_____
_____
_____
_____
_____
_____
_____
_____
_____
_____

Confession

_____
_____
_____
_____
_____
_____
_____
_____
_____
_____

Who He is _____
_____

Prayer

_____
_____
_____
_____
_____
_____
_____
_____
_____
_____

Praise

_____
_____
_____
_____
_____
_____
_____

A WORTHWHILE JOURNEY

*The path of the righteous is like the morning sun,
shining ever brighter till the full light of day.
But the way of the wicked is like deep darkness;
they do not know what makes them stumble.*

Proverbs 4:18-19 NIV

Thought Moment

*"God never said that the journey
would be easy, but He did say that
the arrival would be worthwhile."*
Max Lucado

Biblical Truths _____

_____

_____

_____

_____

_____

_____

_____

Reflection _____

_____

_____

_____

_____

_____

_____

_____

_____

_____

_____

_____

_____

_____

_____

_____

On my heart ♥

_____
_____
_____
_____
_____
_____
_____
_____
_____
_____
_____
_____
_____
_____
_____
_____
_____

Gratitude

_____
_____
_____
_____
_____
_____
_____
_____
_____
_____
_____

Confession

_____
_____
_____
_____
_____
_____
_____
_____
_____
_____
_____

Who He is _____
_____

Prayer

_____
_____
_____
_____
_____
_____
_____
_____
_____

Praise

_____
_____
_____
_____
_____
_____
_____

LIGHT OF THE WORLD

You are the light of the world. A town built on a hill cannot be hidden. Neither do people light a lamp and put it under a bowl. Instead they put it on its stand, and it gives light to everyone in the house.
In the same way, let your light shine before others, that they may see your good deeds and glorify your Father in heaven.

Matthew 5:14-16 NIV

Thought Moment

"Your life as a Christian should make non-believers question their disbelief in God."

Dietrich Bonhoeffer

Biblical Truths _____

_____
_____
_____
_____
_____
_____
_____
_____

Reflection _____

_____
_____
_____
_____
_____
_____
_____
_____
_____
_____
_____
_____
_____
_____
_____
_____

On my heart 🖤

_____
_____
_____
_____
_____
_____
_____
_____
_____
_____
_____
_____
_____
_____
_____
_____
_____
_____
_____

Gratitude

_____
_____
_____
_____
_____
_____
_____
_____
_____
_____
_____

Confession

_____
_____
_____
_____
_____
_____
_____
_____
_____
_____

Who He is

_____

_____

Prayer

_____
_____
_____
_____
_____
_____
_____
_____
_____
_____

Praise

_____
_____
_____
_____
_____
_____
_____
_____

MADE BY GOD & FOR GOD

For everything, absolutely everything,
above and below, visible and invisible,
...everything got started in God and
finds its purpose in him.

Colossians 1:16 MSG

Thought Moment

"You were made by God and for
God, and until you understand
that, life will never make sense."
Rick Warren

Biblical Truths _____

_____
_____
_____
_____
_____
_____
_____

Reflection _____

_____
_____
_____
_____
_____
_____
_____
_____
_____
_____
_____
_____
_____
_____
_____
_____

On my heart ♥

Gratitude

Confession

Who He is

_____

Prayer

_____
_____
_____
_____
_____
_____
_____
_____
_____

Praise

_____
_____
_____
_____
_____
_____
_____

STRENGTH OF FAITHFULNESS

If you are faithful in little things, you will be faithful in large ones.

Luke 16:10a NLT

Thought Moment

"Be faithful in small things because it is in them that your strength lies."

Mother Teresa

Biblical Truths _____

_____
_____
_____
_____
_____
_____
_____

Reflection _____

_____
_____
_____
_____
_____
_____
_____
_____
_____
_____
_____
_____
_____
_____

On my heart ♥

_____
_____
_____
_____
_____
_____
_____
_____
_____
_____
_____
_____
_____
_____
_____
_____
_____

Gratitude

_____
_____
_____
_____
_____
_____
_____
_____
_____
_____
_____
_____

Confession

_____
_____
_____
_____
_____
_____
_____
_____
_____
_____
_____
_____

Who He is

_____

_____

Prayer

_____
_____
_____
_____
_____
_____
_____
_____
_____

Praise

_____
_____
_____
_____
_____
_____
_____
_____
_____

BRINGING LIGHT TO THE WORLD

So we have stopped evaluating others from a human point of view. At one time we thought of Christ merely from a human point of view. How differently we know him now! This means that anyone who belongs to Christ has become a new person. The old life is gone; a new life has begun!

And all of this is a gift from God, who brought us back to himself through Christ. And God has given us this task of reconciling people to him. For God was in Christ, reconciling the world to himself, no longer counting people's sins against them. And he gave us this wonderful message of reconciliation.

So we are Christ's ambassadors; God is making his appeal through us. We speak for Christ when we plead, "Come back to God!" For God made Christ, who never sinned, to be the offering for our sin, so that we could be made right with God through Christ.

2 Corinthians 5:16-21 NLT

Thought Moment

"In a world of selfishness, greed, inequity, and injustice, believers need to be set apart by their consuming love for God, and their sacrificial love for others. That's the kind of holy living that brings salt and light to this dark, decaying world."

Joni Eareckson Tada

Biblical Truths _____

_____

_____

_____

_____

_____

_____

_____

Reflection _____

_____

_____

_____

_____

_____

_____

_____

_____

_____

_____

_____

_____

_____

_____

On my heart 💗

Gratitude

Confession

Who He is _____
_____

Prayer

_____
_____
_____
_____
_____
_____
_____
_____
_____

Praise

_____
_____
_____
_____
_____
_____
_____

FRUITS OF MATURITY

The wisdom from above is first pure, then peace-loving, gentle, reasonable, full of mercy and good fruits, impartial, free of hypocrisy.

James 3:17 NASB

Thought Moment

"You know you've grown when you truly care about the impact your words and deeds have on others."

Christine Caine

Biblical Truths _____

_____
_____
_____
_____
_____
_____
_____

Reflection _____

_____
_____
_____
_____
_____
_____
_____
_____
_____
_____
_____
_____
_____
_____

On my heart ♥

Gratitude

Confession

Who He is _____
_____

Prayer

_____
_____
_____
_____
_____
_____
_____
_____
_____
_____

Praise

_____
_____
_____
_____
_____
_____
_____

DOING BY FAITH

Now Elisha had said to the woman whose son he had restored to life, "Go away with your family and stay for a while wherever you can, because the Lord has decreed a famine in the land that will last seven years." The woman proceeded to do as the man of God said. She and her family went away and stayed in the land of the Philistines seven years.

At the end of the seven years she came back from the land of the Philistines and went to appeal to the king for her house and land. The king was talking to Gehazi, the servant of the man of God, and had said, "Tell me about all the great things Elisha has done." Just as Gehazi was telling the king how Elisha had restored the dead to life, the woman whose son Elisha had brought back to life came to appeal to the king for her house and land.

Gehazi said, "This is the woman, my lord the king, and this is her son whom Elisha restored to life." The king asked the woman about it, and she told him.

Then he assigned an official to her case and said to him, "Give back everything that belonged to her, including all the income from her land from the day she left the country until now."

2 Kings 8:1-6 NIV

Thought Moment

"Stop looking at what you can't do and find something you can do and start doing it by faith. You know why? If you will do the little bit you can do, God will do everything that you cannot do."

Joyce Meyer

Biblical Truths

_____

_____

_____

_____

_____

_____

_____

_____

_____

Reflection

_____

_____

_____

_____

_____

_____

_____

_____

_____

_____

_____

_____

_____

_____

_____

_____

On my heart 🖤

_____
_____
_____
_____
_____
_____
_____
_____
_____
_____
_____
_____
_____
_____
_____
_____

Gratitude

_____
_____
_____
_____
_____
_____
_____
_____
_____
_____

Confession

_____
_____
_____
_____
_____
_____
_____
_____
_____
_____
_____

Who He is

_____

_____

Prayer

_____

_____

_____

_____

_____

_____

_____

_____

_____

_____

Praise

_____

_____

_____

_____

_____

_____

_____

_____

OWNING MISTAKES

A man who refuses to admit his mistakes can never be successful. But if he confesses and forsakes them, he gets another chance.

Proverbs 28:13 TLB

 — Thought Moment —

"When you own a mistake it no longer owns you."

Lisa Bevere

Biblical Truths _____

_____

_____

_____

_____

_____

_____

_____

Reflection _____

_____

_____

_____

_____

_____

_____

_____

_____

_____

_____

_____

_____

_____

_____

On my heart 🖤

_____
_____
_____
_____
_____
_____
_____
_____
_____
_____
_____
_____
_____
_____
_____
_____
_____

Gratitude

_____
_____
_____
_____
_____
_____
_____
_____
_____
_____
_____
_____
_____

Confession

_____
_____
_____
_____
_____
_____
_____
_____
_____
_____
_____
_____
_____

Who He is _____

_____

Prayer

_____
_____
_____
_____
_____
_____
_____
_____
_____
_____

Praise

_____
_____
_____
_____
_____
_____
_____
_____
_____

TEARING DOWN STRONGHOLDS

Do not conform to the pattern of this world, but be transformed by the renewing of your mind. Then you will be able to test and approve what God's will is—his good, pleasing and perfect will.

Romans 12:2 NIV

One who is wise can go up against the city of the mighty and pull down the stronghold in which they trust.

Proverbs 21:22 NIV

Thought Moment

"When a stronghold is built in the mind, what is at stake is the mind having the knowledge of God in it. The stronghold exists as protection from something dangerous coming in; however, it is the very thing that keeps the knowledge of God out. Tear them down with the truth about Christ, by the Spirit, as revealed in the Scriptures. Every brick has to go so that the Christ, the King of glory, can come in."

Jackie Hill Perry, <u>Upon Waking</u>

Biblical Truths _____

_____
_____
_____
_____
_____
_____
_____

Reflection _____

_____
_____
_____
_____
_____
_____
_____
_____
_____
_____
_____
_____
_____
_____

On my heart ♥

_____
_____
_____
_____
_____
_____
_____
_____
_____
_____
_____
_____
_____
_____
_____
_____
_____

Gratitude

_____
_____
_____
_____
_____
_____
_____
_____
_____
_____

Confession

_____
_____
_____
_____
_____
_____
_____
_____
_____

Who He is

_____

_____

Prayer

_____
_____
_____
_____
_____
_____
_____
_____
_____
_____

Praise

_____
_____
_____
_____
_____
_____
_____
_____

TESTING OF OUR FAITH

*Consider it all joy, my brothers and sisters,
when you encounter various trials,
knowing that the testing of your faith produces
endurance.
And let endurance have its perfect result, so
that you may be perfect and complete,
lacking in nothing.*

James 1:2-3 NASB

Thought Moment

"Your sufferings are not meant to defeat you. God allows those sufferings so that your soul might be more courageous."

Joni Eareckson Tada

Biblical Truths

_____

_____

_____

_____

_____

_____

_____

_____

Reflection

_____

_____

_____

_____

_____

_____

_____

_____

_____

_____

_____

_____

_____

_____

_____

On my heart ♥

_____
_____
_____
_____
_____
_____
_____
_____
_____
_____
_____
_____
_____
_____
_____
_____
_____
_____
_____
_____

Gratitude

_____
_____
_____
_____
_____
_____
_____
_____
_____
_____
_____
_____
_____

Confession

_____
_____
_____
_____
_____
_____
_____
_____
_____
_____

Who He is _____
_____

Prayer

_____
_____
_____
_____
_____
_____
_____
_____
_____
_____
_____

Praise

_____
_____
_____
_____
_____
_____
_____
_____
_____

CHARACTER OVER COMFORT

Teach me your way, Lord; lead me in a straight path
because of my oppressors.
Do not turn me over to the desire of my foes, for false witnesses rise up
against me, spouting malicious accusations.
I remain confident of this:
I will see the goodness of the Lord in the land of the living.
Wait for the Lord; be strong and take heart
and wait for the Lord.

Psalm 27:11-14 NIV

Thought Moment

"Life is a series of problems: Either you are in one now, you're just coming out of one, or you're getting ready to go into another one. The reason for this is that God is more interested in your character than your comfort. God is more interested in making your life holy than He is in making your life happy. We can be reasonably happy here on earth, but that's not the goal in life. The goal is to grow in character, in Christ likeness."

Rick Warren

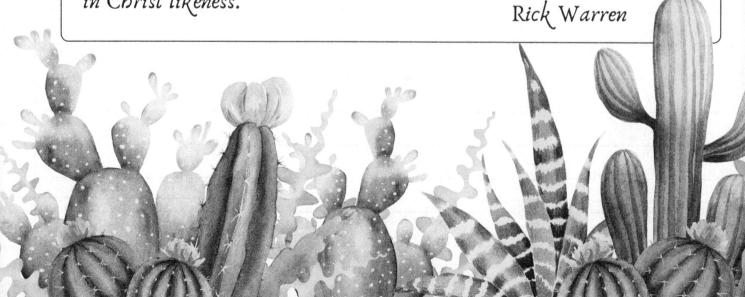

Biblical Truths _____

_____
_____
_____
_____
_____
_____
_____

Reflection _____

_____
_____
_____
_____
_____
_____
_____
_____
_____
_____
_____
_____
_____
_____

On my heart ♥

_____
_____
_____
_____
_____
_____
_____
_____
_____
_____
_____
_____
_____
_____
_____
_____
_____

Gratitude

_____
_____
_____
_____
_____
_____
_____
_____
_____
_____
_____

Confession

_____
_____
_____
_____
_____
_____
_____
_____
_____
_____

Who He is _____

Prayer

_____
_____
_____
_____
_____
_____
_____
_____

Praise

_____
_____
_____
_____
_____
_____

SUCCESS ISN'T DEPENDENT ON US

Then Moses summoned Joshua. He said to him with all Israel watching, "Be strong. Take courage. You will enter the land with this people, this land that God promised their ancestors that he'd give them. You will make them the proud possessors of it. God is striding ahead of you. He's right there with you. He won't let you down; he won't leave you. Don't be intimidated. Don't worry."

Deuteronomy 31:7-8 MSG

Thought Moment

"Fear arises when we imagine that everything depends on us."

Elisabeth Elliot

Biblical Truths _____

_____
_____
_____
_____
_____
_____
_____

Reflection _____

_____
_____
_____
_____
_____
_____
_____
_____
_____
_____
_____
_____
_____
_____
_____

On my heart ♥

_____
_____
_____
_____
_____
_____
_____
_____
_____
_____
_____
_____
_____
_____
_____
_____
_____

Gratitude

_____
_____
_____
_____
_____
_____
_____
_____
_____
_____
_____

Confession

_____
_____
_____
_____
_____
_____
_____
_____
_____
_____
_____

Who He is _____
_____

Prayer

_____
_____
_____
_____
_____
_____
_____
_____
_____
_____
_____
_____

Praise

_____
_____
_____
_____
_____
_____
_____
_____

Who He is

POWER AND AUTHORITY

Do you not know that you are a temple of God and that the Spirit of God dwells in you? If anyone destroys the temple of God, God will destroy that person; for the temple of God is holy, and that is what you are.

1 Corinthians 3:16-17 NASB

Thought Moment

"No matter what is against you, it is no match for the power and authority He's given you access to. There may be armies standing against you, but they're only waiting to become an unwitting witness to the overcoming power of God and the overriding ocean of His grace."
Priscilla Shirer, <u>Fervent</u>

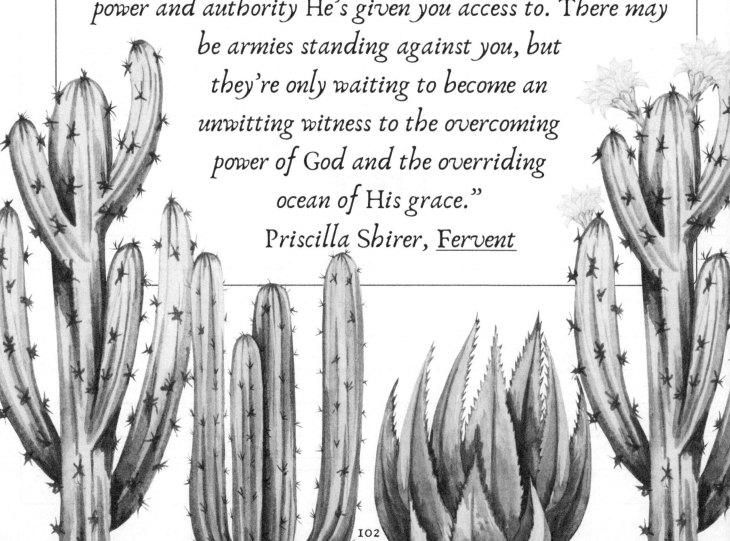

Biblical Truths _____

_____

_____

_____

_____

_____

_____

_____

Reflection _____

_____

_____

_____

_____

_____

_____

_____

_____

_____

_____

_____

_____

_____

On my heart 🖤

_____
_____
_____
_____
_____
_____
_____
_____
_____
_____
_____
_____
_____
_____
_____
_____
_____

Gratitude

_____
_____
_____
_____
_____
_____
_____
_____
_____
_____
_____
_____

Confession

_____
_____
_____
_____
_____
_____
_____
_____
_____

Who He is _____
_____

Prayer

_____
_____
_____
_____
_____
_____
_____
_____
_____
_____

Praise

_____
_____
_____
_____
_____
_____
_____
_____

HE SPECIALIZES IN THE IMPOSSIBLE

Is anyone among you suffering? Then he must pray. Is anyone cheerful? He is to sing praises. Is anyone among you sick? Then he must call for the elders of the church and they are to pray over him, anointing him with oil in the name of the Lord; and the prayer of faith will restore the one who is sick, and the Lord will raise him up, and if he has committed sins, they will be forgiven him. Therefore, confess your sins to one another, and pray for one another so that you may be healed. A prayer of a righteous person, when it is brought about, can accomplish much.

James 5:13-16 NASB

Thought Moment

"The wonderful thing about praying is that you leave a world of not being able to do something and enter God's realm where everything is possible. He specializes in the impossible. Nothing is too great for His almighty power. Nothing is too small for His love."

Corrie ten Boom

Biblical Truths _____

_____

_____

_____

_____

_____

_____

_____

Reflection _____

_____

_____

_____

_____

_____

_____

_____

_____

_____

_____

_____

_____

_____

_____

_____

On my heart ♥

_____
_____
_____
_____
_____
_____
_____
_____
_____
_____
_____
_____
_____
_____
_____
_____
_____
_____
_____

Gratitude

_____
_____
_____
_____
_____
_____
_____
_____
_____
_____
_____
_____

Confession

_____
_____
_____
_____
_____
_____
_____
_____
_____
_____

Who He is

_____

_____

Prayer

_____
_____
_____
_____
_____
_____
_____
_____
_____
_____

Praise

_____
_____
_____
_____
_____
_____
_____

MAKE HIM YOUR LORD

If my people, who are called by my name, will humble themselves and pray and seek my face and turn from their wicked ways, then I will hear from heaven, and I will forgive their sin and will heal their land.

2 Chronicles 7:14 NIV

Thought Moment

"It's not enough to confess Jesus as Savior. You must make Him your Lord. Savior is the benefit you receive. Lord is the position He is to be given."

John Bevere

Biblical Truths _____

_____
_____
_____
_____
_____
_____
_____

Reflection _____

_____
_____
_____
_____
_____
_____
_____
_____
_____
_____
_____
_____
_____
_____

On my heart ♥

_____
_____
_____
_____
_____
_____
_____
_____
_____
_____
_____
_____
_____
_____
_____
_____
_____
_____

Gratitude

_____
_____
_____
_____
_____
_____
_____
_____
_____
_____
_____
_____

Confession

_____
_____
_____
_____
_____
_____
_____
_____
_____
_____

Who He is

_____

Prayer

_____
_____
_____
_____
_____
_____
_____
_____
_____

Praise

_____
_____
_____
_____
_____
_____
_____
_____

MY MOUTH WILL PRAISE HIM

The Lord is righteous in all His ways,
And kind in all His works.
The Lord is near to all who call on Him,
To all who call on Him in truth.
He will fulfill the desire of those who fear Him;
He will also hear their cry for help and save them.
The Lord watches over all who love Him,
But He will destroy all the wicked.
My mouth will speak the praise of the Lord,
And all flesh will bless His holy name forever and ever.

Psalm 145:17-21 NASB

Thought Moment

"It is not the trials in your life that develop or destroy you, but rather your response to those hardships."

Charles Stanley

Biblical Truths _____

_____

_____

_____

_____

_____

_____

_____

Reflection _____

_____

_____

_____

_____

_____

_____

_____

_____

_____

_____

_____

_____

_____

_____

_____

On my heart ♥

_____
_____
_____
_____
_____
_____
_____
_____
_____
_____
_____
_____
_____
_____
_____
_____
_____
_____

Gratitude

_____
_____
_____
_____
_____
_____
_____
_____
_____
_____
_____
_____
_____

Confession

_____
_____
_____
_____
_____
_____
_____
_____
_____
_____

Who He is _____

_____

Prayer

_____
_____
_____
_____
_____
_____
_____
_____
_____
_____
_____

Praise

_____
_____
_____
_____
_____
_____
_____
_____
_____

SUBMISSION

God is opposed to the proud, but gives grace to the humble. Submit therefore to God. But resist the devil, and he will flee from you. Come close to God and He will come close to you.

James 4:6b-8 NASB

Thought Moment

"Submission involves getting rid of everything which hinders God's control over our lives."

Billy Graham

Biblical Truths _____

_____

_____

_____

_____

_____

_____

Reflection _____

_____

_____

_____

_____

_____

_____

_____

_____

_____

_____

_____

_____

_____

On my heart

Gratitude

Confession

Who He is _____

Prayer

_____
_____
_____
_____
_____
_____
_____
_____
_____
_____

Praise

_____
_____
_____
_____
_____
_____
_____
_____

IF TODAY WAS YOUR LAST

Be very careful, then, how you live—not as unwise but as wise,
making the most of every opportunity,
because the days are evil.
Therefore do not be foolish,
but understand what the Lord's will is.
Be filled with the Spirit, speaking to one another with psalms,
hymns, and songs from the Spirit.
Sing and make music from your heart to the Lord, always
giving thanks to God the Father for everything,
in the name of our Lord Jesus Christ.

Ephesians 5:15-17, 18b-20 NIV

Thought Moment

"If today were your last, would you do what you're doing? Or would you love more, give more, forgive more? Then do so! Forgive and give as if it were your last opportunity. Love like there's no tomorrow, and if tomorrow comes, love again."

Max Lucado

Week: _____

Biblical Truths _____

_____
_____
_____
_____
_____
_____
_____

Reflection _____

_____
_____
_____
_____
_____
_____
_____
_____
_____
_____
_____
_____
_____
_____
_____
_____

On my heart ♥

_____
_____
_____
_____
_____
_____
_____
_____
_____
_____
_____
_____
_____
_____
_____
_____
_____

Gratitude

_____
_____
_____
_____
_____
_____
_____
_____
_____
_____
_____

Confession

_____
_____
_____
_____
_____
_____
_____
_____
_____
_____

Who He is _____
_____

Prayer

_____
_____
_____
_____
_____
_____
_____
_____
_____
_____

Praise

_____
_____
_____
_____
_____
_____
_____
_____

FAITH BUILT UPON JESUS

Let's run with endurance the race that is set before us, looking only at Jesus, the originator and perfecter of the faith, who for the joy set before Him endured the cross, despising the shame, and has sat down at the right hand of the throne of God.
For consider Him who has endured such hostility by sinners against Himself, so that you will not grow weary and lose heart.

Hebrews 12:1b-3 NASB

Thought Moment

Oswald Chambers taught how Peter, having disowned Jesus with vehement words and curses, found himself at the brink of his own limitations and self-assuredness. It was at this point of destitution that he was most ready to accept the profound gift from the resurrected Jesus—the Holy Spirit.

In your spiritual journey, remember that your foundation is not the changes God has made in you, for this leads quickly to the end of oneself. Rather, your faith must be built upon Jesus Christ and the Holy Spirit He gives. Let this be the cornerstone of your spiritual walk and understanding.

Biblical Truths _____

_____

_____

_____

_____

_____

_____

_____

Reflection _____

_____

_____

_____

_____

_____

_____

_____

_____

_____

_____

_____

_____

_____

_____

On my heart 🖤

_____
_____
_____
_____
_____
_____
_____
_____
_____
_____
_____
_____
_____
_____
_____
_____
_____

Gratitude

_____
_____
_____
_____
_____
_____
_____
_____
_____
_____
_____

Confession

_____
_____
_____
_____
_____
_____
_____
_____
_____
_____

Who He is

_____

Prayer

_____
_____
_____
_____
_____
_____
_____
_____
_____
_____
_____

Praise

_____
_____
_____
_____
_____
_____
_____
_____

DOERS OF THE WORD

Now everyone must be quick to hear, slow to speak, and slow to anger; for a man's anger does not bring about the righteousness of God.
Therefore, ridding yourselves of all filthiness and all that remains of wickedness, in humility receive the word implanted,
which is able to save your souls.
But prove yourselves doers of the word, and not just hearers who deceive themselves. For if anyone is a hearer of the word and not a doer, he is like a man who looks at his natural face in a mirror; for once he has looked at himself and gone away, he has immediately forgotten what kind of person he was.
But one who has looked intently at the perfect law, the law of freedom, and has continued in it, not having become a forgetful hearer but an active doer, this person will be blessed in what he does.

James 1:19b-25 NASB

Thought Moment

"'If Christianity is valid, why is there so much evil in the world?' To this the famous preacher replied, 'With so much soap, why are there so many dirty people in the world? Christianity, like soap, must be personally applied if it is to make a difference in our lives'."

Billy Graham

Biblical Truths _____

_____
_____
_____
_____
_____
_____
_____

Reflection _____

_____
_____
_____
_____
_____
_____
_____
_____
_____
_____
_____
_____
_____
_____

On my heart ♥

_____
_____
_____
_____
_____
_____
_____
_____
_____
_____
_____
_____
_____
_____
_____
_____
_____
_____

Gratitude

_____
_____
_____
_____
_____
_____
_____
_____
_____
_____
_____

Confession

_____
_____
_____
_____
_____
_____
_____
_____
_____
_____

Who He is _____

_____

Prayer

_____

_____

_____

_____

_____

_____

_____

_____

_____

_____

_____

_____

Praise

_____

_____

_____

_____

_____

_____

_____

_____

_____

BE KIND & COMPASSIONATE

Do not let any unwholesome talk come out of your mouths, but only what is helpful for building others up according to their needs, that it may benefit those who listen.

Be kind and compassionate to one another, forgiving each other, just as in Christ God forgave you.

Ephesians 4:29, 32 NIV

Thought Moment

"We must learn to regard people less in the light of what they do or omit to do, and more in the light of what they suffer."

Dietrich Bonhoeffer

Week: _____

Biblical Truths _____

_____
_____
_____
_____
_____
_____
_____

Reflection _____

_____
_____
_____
_____
_____
_____
_____
_____
_____
_____
_____
_____
_____
_____
_____

On my heart ♥

_____
_____
_____
_____
_____
_____
_____
_____
_____
_____
_____
_____
_____
_____
_____
_____

Gratitude

_____
_____
_____
_____
_____
_____
_____
_____
_____
_____

Confession

_____
_____
_____
_____
_____
_____
_____
_____
_____

Who He is _____

_____

_____

Prayer

_____

_____

_____

_____

_____

_____

_____

_____

_____

Praise

_____

_____

_____

_____

_____

_____

_____

_____

DAILY ACTS OF WORSHIP

Make sure you don't take things for granted and go slack in working for the common good; share what you have with others. God takes particular pleasure in acts of worship—a different kind of "sacrifice"— that take place in kitchen and workplace and on the streets.

Hebrews 13:16 MSG

Thought Moment

"Do not wait for leaders; do it alone, person to person."

Mother Teresa

Biblical Truths _____

_____
_____
_____
_____
_____
_____
_____
_____

Reflection _____

_____
_____
_____
_____
_____
_____
_____
_____
_____
_____
_____
_____
_____
_____
_____
_____
_____

On my heart ♥

_____
_____
_____
_____
_____
_____
_____
_____
_____
_____
_____
_____
_____
_____
_____
_____
_____
_____

Gratitude

_____
_____
_____
_____
_____
_____
_____
_____
_____
_____
_____

Confession

_____
_____
_____
_____
_____
_____
_____
_____
_____
_____
_____

Who He is

_____

_____

Prayer

_____

_____

_____

_____

_____

_____

_____

_____

_____

Praise

_____

_____

_____

_____

_____

_____

_____

_____

A CHILD OF THE LIGHT

For once you were full of darkness, but now you have light from the Lord. So live as people of light! For this light within you produces only what is good and right and true. Carefully determine what pleases the Lord.

Ephesians 5:8-10 NLT

Thought Moment

"You are the only Bible some unbelievers will ever read."

John MacArthur

Week: _____

Biblical Truths _____

_____
_____
_____
_____
_____
_____
_____
_____

Reflection _____

_____
_____
_____
_____
_____
_____
_____
_____
_____
_____
_____
_____
_____
_____
_____

On my heart 🖤

_____

_____

_____

_____

_____

_____

_____

_____

_____

_____

_____

_____

_____

_____

_____

_____

Gratitude

_____

_____

_____

_____

_____

_____

_____

_____

_____

Confession

_____

_____

_____

_____

_____

_____

_____

_____

_____

Who He is _____
_____

Prayer

_____
_____
_____
_____
_____
_____
_____
_____
_____
_____

Praise

_____
_____
_____
_____
_____
_____
_____
_____
_____

FOCUSING ON JESUS

For God so loved the world, that He gave His only Son, so that everyone who believes in Him will not perish, but have eternal life. For God did not send the Son into the world to judge the world, but so that the world might be saved through Him. The one who believes in Him is not judged; the one who does not believe has been judged already, because he has not believed in the name of the only Son of God. And this is the judgment, that the Light has come into the world, and people loved the darkness rather than the Light; for their deeds were evil. For everyone who does evil hates the Light, and does not come to the Light, so that his deeds will not be exposed. But the one who practices the truth comes to the Light, so that his deeds will be revealed as having been performed in God.

John 3:16-21 NASB

Thought Moment

"We need to stop making what people did to us bigger than what Jesus did for us."

Christine Caine

Biblical Truths _____

_____
_____
_____
_____
_____
_____
_____
_____

Reflection _____

_____
_____
_____
_____
_____
_____
_____
_____
_____
_____
_____
_____
_____
_____
_____
_____

On my heart ♥

Gratitude

Confession

Who He is

_____

_____

Prayer

_____
_____
_____
_____
_____
_____
_____
_____
_____
_____

Praise

_____
_____
_____
_____
_____
_____
_____
_____

SHOUT FOR JOY TO THE LORD

Shout for joy to the Lord, all the earth.
Worship the Lord with gladness;
come before him with joyful songs.
Know that the Lord is God.
It is he who made us, and we are his;
we are his people, the sheep of his pasture.
Enter his gates with thanksgiving
and his courts with praise;
give thanks to him and praise his name.
For the Lord is good and his love endures forever;
his faithfulness continues
through all generations.

Psalms 100 NIV

Thought Moment

"There's no happier person than a truly thankful, content person."

Joyce Meyer

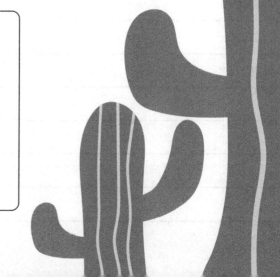

150

Biblical Truths _____

_____

_____

_____

_____

_____

_____

_____

Reflection _____

_____

_____

_____

_____

_____

_____

_____

_____

_____

_____

_____

_____

_____

On my heart 🖤

_____
_____
_____
_____
_____
_____
_____
_____
_____
_____
_____
_____
_____
_____
_____
_____
_____
_____

Gratitude

_____
_____
_____
_____
_____
_____
_____
_____
_____
_____
_____

Confession

_____
_____
_____
_____
_____
_____
_____
_____
_____
_____

Who He is _____

Prayer

_____
_____
_____
_____
_____
_____
_____
_____
_____
_____

Praise

_____
_____
_____
_____
_____
_____
_____
_____

TIME TO DO THE WILL OF GOD

As Jesus and his disciples were on their way, he came to a village where a woman named Martha opened her home to him. She had a sister called Mary, who sat at the Lord's feet listening to what he said. But Martha was distracted by all the preparations that had to be made. She came to him and asked, "Lord, don't you care that my sister has left me to do the work by myself? Tell her to help me!"

"Martha, Martha," the Lord answered, "you are worried and upset about many things, but few things are needed—or indeed only one. Mary has chosen what is better, and it will not be taken away from her."

Luke 10:38-42 NIV

Thought Moment

"If we really have too much to do, there are some items on the agenda which God did not put there. Let us submit the list to Him and ask Him to indicate which items we must delete. There is always time to do the will of God. If we are too busy to do that, we are too busy."

Elisabeth Elliot

Biblical Truths _____

_____
_____
_____
_____
_____
_____
_____

Reflection _____

_____
_____
_____
_____
_____
_____
_____
_____
_____
_____
_____
_____
_____
_____
_____

On my heart ♥

_____
_____
_____
_____
_____
_____
_____
_____
_____
_____
_____
_____
_____
_____
_____

Gratitude

_____
_____
_____
_____
_____
_____
_____
_____
_____
_____
_____

Confession

_____
_____
_____
_____
_____
_____
_____
_____
_____
_____

Who He is _____
_____

Prayer

_____
_____
_____
_____
_____
_____
_____
_____
_____
_____
_____

Praise

_____
_____
_____
_____
_____
_____
_____
_____

THE FIGHT OF GOD'S SPIRIT IN YOU

The Lord is my light and my salvation—whom shall I fear?
The Lord is the stronghold of my life—of whom shall I be afraid?
When the wicked advance against me to devour me,
it is my enemies and my foes who will stumble and fall.
Though an army besiege me, my heart will not fear;
though war break out against me, even then I will be confident.

One thing I ask from the Lord, this only do I seek:
that I may dwell in the house of the Lord all the days of my life,
to gaze on the beauty of the Lord and to seek him in his temple.
For in the day of trouble he will keep me safe in his dwelling;
he will hide me in the shelter of his sacred tent and set me high upon a rock.
Then my head will be exalted above the enemies who surround me;
at his sacred tent I will sacrifice with shouts of joy; I will sing and make music to the Lord.

Psalm 23:1-6 NIV

Thought Moment

"At the end of the day, the enemy is going to be sorry he ever messed with you. You're about to become his worst nightmare a million times over. He thought he could wear you down, sure that after a while you'd give up without much of a fight. Well, just wait till he encounters the fight of God's Spirit in you. Because... This. Means. War."

Priscilla Shirer, _Fervent_

Week: _____

Biblical Truths _____

_____
_____
_____
_____
_____
_____
_____

Reflection _____

_____
_____
_____
_____
_____
_____
_____
_____
_____
_____
_____
_____
_____
_____
_____

On my heart ♥

_____
_____
_____
_____
_____
_____
_____
_____
_____
_____
_____
_____
_____
_____
_____
_____
_____
_____

Gratitude

_____
_____
_____
_____
_____
_____
_____
_____
_____
_____
_____
_____

Confession

_____
_____
_____
_____
_____
_____
_____
_____
_____

Who He is _____

_____

Prayer

_____
_____
_____
_____
_____
_____
_____
_____
_____
_____
_____

Praise

_____
_____
_____
_____
_____
_____
_____
_____
_____
_____

SIT STILL AND TRUST

"I will bring my people Israel back from exile.
They will rebuild the ruined cities and live in them.
They will plant vineyards and drink their wine;
they will make gardens and eat their fruit.
I will plant Israel in their own land,
never again to be uprooted
from the land I have given them,"
says the Lord your God.

Amos 9:14-15 NIV

Thought Moment

"When a train goes through a tunnel and it gets dark, you don't throw away the ticket and jump off. You sit still and trust the engineer."

Corrie ten Boom

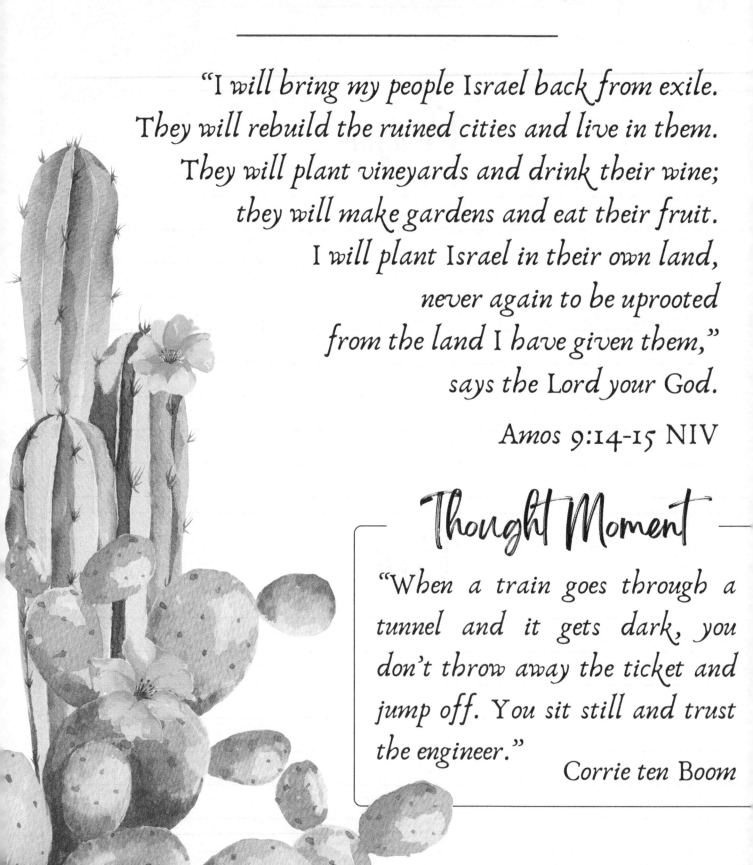

Biblical Truths _____

_____
_____
_____
_____
_____
_____
_____
_____

Reflection _____

_____
_____
_____
_____
_____
_____
_____
_____
_____
_____
_____
_____
_____
_____
_____
_____

On my heart 🖤

_____
_____
_____
_____
_____
_____
_____
_____
_____
_____
_____
_____
_____
_____
_____
_____

Gratitude

_____
_____
_____
_____
_____
_____
_____
_____
_____
_____
_____

Confession

_____
_____
_____
_____
_____
_____
_____
_____
_____

Who He is _____

_____

Prayer

_____

_____

_____

_____

_____

_____

_____

_____

_____

_____

_____

Praise

_____

_____

_____

_____

_____

_____

_____

_____

TAKE THE NEXT STEP

Have I not commanded you? Be strong and courageous! Do not be terrified nor dismayed, for the Lord your God is with you wherever you go.

Joshua 1:9 NASB

—  —

"Faith isn't the ability to believe long and far into the misty future. It's simply taking God at His Word and taking the next step."

Joni Eareckson Tada

Week: _____

Biblical Truths _____

_____
_____
_____
_____
_____
_____
_____

Reflection _____

_____
_____
_____
_____
_____
_____
_____
_____
_____
_____
_____
_____
_____
_____
_____
_____

On my heart ♥

_____

_____

_____

_____

_____

_____

_____

_____

_____

_____

_____

_____

_____

_____

_____

_____

_____

_____

_____

Gratitude

_____

_____

_____

_____

_____

_____

_____

_____

_____

_____

Confession

_____

_____

_____

_____

_____

_____

_____

_____

_____

_____

_____

Who He is

_____

Prayer

_____
_____
_____
_____
_____
_____
_____
_____
_____

Praise

_____
_____
_____
_____
_____
_____
_____
_____

LOOKING TO WHAT GOD SEES

But if any of you lacks wisdom, let him ask of God, who gives to all generously and without reproach, and it will be given to him. But he must ask in faith without any doubting, for the one who doubts is like the surf of the sea, driven and tossed by the wind.

James 1:5-6 NASB

Thought Moment

"Trusting God means looking beyond what we can see to what God sees."

Charles Stanley

Biblical Truths _____

_____

_____

_____

_____

_____

_____

_____

Reflection _____

_____

_____

_____

_____

_____

_____

_____

_____

_____

_____

_____

_____

_____

_____

_____

On my heart ♥

_____
_____
_____
_____
_____
_____
_____
_____
_____
_____
_____
_____
_____
_____
_____
_____
_____

Gratitude

_____
_____
_____
_____
_____
_____
_____
_____
_____
_____
_____

Confession

_____
_____
_____
_____
_____
_____
_____
_____
_____

Who He is _____

Prayer

_____
_____
_____
_____
_____
_____
_____
_____
_____
_____

Praise

_____
_____
_____
_____
_____
_____
_____
_____

REDEEMER & RESTORER

I delight greatly in the Lord; my soul rejoices in my God.
For he has clothed me with garments of salvation and arrayed me in a robe of
his righteousness, as a bridegroom adorns his head like a priest, and as a bride
adorns herself with her jewels.

Isaiah 61:10 NIV

Thought Moment

Dr. Sherri Yoder shares a powerful message of hope and redemption, reminding us that even when we feel utterly defeated and believe that a fulfilling life is beyond our reach, we should not give up.

She confesses to having felt broken and unworthy, tempted to surrender to despair. In her darkest moments, it was the gentle urging of Jesus to seek Him that sparked a change.

Yoder emphasizes that it was not through her own strength but through a heartfelt pursuit of God, despite feeling forsaken and overwhelmed by her failures, that she found renewal. She credits God's mercy for not abandoning her to her despair but instead guiding her towards healing and transformation.

Through consistent prayer, engagement with scripture, and worship, Yoder experienced a profound shift from resistance to surrender, leading her out of a self-imposed prison towards a life marked by God's redeeming love. This journey, though challenging and without immediate resolution, gradually unveiled the presence of a God eager to redeem and restore.

Biblical Truths _____

_____
_____
_____
_____
_____
_____
_____
_____

Reflection _____

_____
_____
_____
_____
_____
_____
_____
_____
_____
_____
_____
_____
_____
_____
_____
_____
_____

On my heart ♥

_____
_____
_____
_____
_____
_____
_____
_____
_____
_____
_____
_____
_____
_____
_____
_____
_____

Gratitude

_____
_____
_____
_____
_____
_____
_____
_____
_____
_____
_____
_____

Confession

_____
_____
_____
_____
_____
_____
_____
_____
_____
_____
_____

Who He is _____

_____

Prayer

_____
_____
_____
_____
_____
_____
_____
_____
_____
_____
_____
_____

Praise

_____
_____
_____
_____
_____
_____
_____
_____

WORDS REVEAL CHARACTER

For every species of beasts and birds, of reptiles and creatures of the sea, is tamed and has been tamed by the human race. But no one among mankind can tame the tongue; it is a restless evil, full of deadly poison. With it we bless our Lord and Father, and with it we curse people, who have been made in the likeness of God; from the same mouth come both blessing and cursing. My brothers and sisters, these things should not be this way.

James 3:7-10 NASB

Thought Moment

"We need to think of our tongue as a messenger that runs errands for our heart. Our words reveal our character."

Charles Swindoll

Biblical Truths _____

_____
_____
_____
_____
_____
_____
_____

Reflection _____

_____
_____
_____
_____
_____
_____
_____
_____
_____
_____
_____
_____
_____
_____
_____

On my heart ♥

Gratitude

Confession

Who He is _____

_____

Prayer

_____
_____
_____
_____
_____
_____
_____
_____
_____

Praise

_____
_____
_____
_____
_____
_____
_____
_____

HIS LOVE ENDURES FOREVER

Give thanks to the Lord, for he is good. His love endures forever.
Give thanks to the God of gods. His love endures forever.
Give thanks to the Lord of lords: His love endures forever.
To him who alone does great wonders,
His love endures forever.
Who by his understanding made the heavens,
His love endures forever.
Who spread out the earth upon the waters,
His love endures forever.
Who made the great lights—His love endures forever.
The sun to govern the day, His love endures forever.
The moon and stars to govern the night;
His love endures forever.
Psalm 136:1-9 NIV

Thought Moment

"The great thing to remember is that though our feelings come and go, His love for us does not."

C. S. Lewis

Biblical Truths _____

_____
_____
_____
_____
_____
_____
_____
_____

Reflection _____

_____
_____
_____
_____
_____
_____
_____
_____
_____
_____
_____
_____
_____
_____
_____
_____

On my heart ♥

_____
_____
_____
_____
_____
_____
_____
_____
_____
_____
_____
_____
_____
_____
_____
_____

Gratitude

_____
_____
_____
_____
_____
_____
_____
_____
_____
_____

Confession

_____
_____
_____
_____
_____
_____
_____
_____
_____

Who He is _____

_____

Prayer

_____

_____

_____

_____

_____

_____

_____

_____

_____

_____

Praise

_____

_____

_____

_____

_____

_____

_____

_____

MORE THAN CONQUERORS

No, *in all these things we are more than conquerors through him who loved us. For I am convinced that neither death nor life, neither angels nor demons, neither the present nor the future, nor any powers, neither height nor depth, nor anything else in all creation, will be able to separate us from the love of God that is in Christ Jesus our Lord.*

Romans 8:37-39 NIV

Thought Moment

"Stop calling yourself ordinary. Because of the blood of Christ and the power of the Holy Spirit, you are extraordinary!"

Robert Morris

Biblical Truths _____

_____

_____

_____

_____

_____

_____

_____

Reflection _____

_____

_____

_____

_____

_____

_____

_____

_____

_____

_____

_____

_____

_____

_____

On my heart ♥

_____
_____
_____
_____
_____
_____
_____
_____
_____
_____
_____
_____
_____
_____
_____
_____
_____
_____
_____

Gratitude

_____
_____
_____
_____
_____
_____
_____
_____
_____
_____
_____
_____
_____

Confession

_____
_____
_____
_____
_____
_____
_____
_____
_____
_____

Who He is _____
_____

Prayer

_____
_____
_____
_____
_____
_____
_____
_____
_____

Praise

_____
_____
_____
_____
_____
_____
_____
_____

HE LOVES THE LOWLY & LOST

I *will search for the lost and bring back the strays. I will bind up the injured and strengthen the weak, but the sleek and the strong I will destroy. I will shepherd the flock with justice.*

Ezekiel 34:16 NIV

Thought Moment

"Wonder of all wonders, God loves the lowly...God is near to lowliness; he loves the lost, the neglected, the unseemly, the excluded, the weak and broken."

Dietrich Bonhoeffer

Biblical Truths _____

_____
_____
_____
_____
_____
_____
_____
_____

Reflection _____

_____
_____
_____
_____
_____
_____
_____
_____
_____
_____
_____
_____
_____
_____
_____
_____

On my heart ♥

Gratitude

Confession

Who He is _____

_____

Prayer

_____
_____
_____
_____
_____
_____
_____
_____
_____
_____

Praise

_____
_____
_____
_____
_____
_____
_____

LOVING INSTEAD OF JUDGING

Don't pick on people, jump on their failures, criticize their faults—unless, of course, you want the same treatment. That critical spirit has a way of boomeranging. It's easy to see a smudge on your neighbor's face and be oblivious to the ugly sneer on your own. Do you have the nerve to say, 'Let me wash your face for you,' when your own face is distorted by contempt? It's this whole traveling road-show mentality all over again, playing a holier-than-thou part instead of just living your part. Wipe that ugly sneer off your own face, and you might be fit to offer a washcloth to your neighbor.

Matthew 7:1-5 MSG

Thought Moment

"If you judge people, you have no time to love them."
Mother Teresa

Biblical Truths _____

_____
_____
_____
_____
_____
_____
_____

Reflection

_____
_____
_____
_____
_____
_____
_____
_____
_____
_____
_____
_____
_____
_____

On my heart ♥

_____
_____
_____
_____
_____
_____
_____
_____
_____
_____
_____
_____
_____
_____
_____
_____
_____
_____
_____
_____

Gratitude

_____
_____
_____
_____
_____
_____
_____
_____
_____
_____
_____
_____
_____

Confession

_____
_____
_____
_____
_____
_____
_____
_____
_____
_____
_____

Who He is _____

Prayer

_____
_____
_____
_____
_____
_____
_____
_____
_____
_____

Praise

_____
_____
_____
_____
_____
_____
_____
_____

MAKING YOU A CHAMPION

Do you not know? Have you not heard?
The Lord is the everlasting God,
the Creator of the ends of the earth.
He will not grow tired or weary,
and his understanding no one can fathom.
He gives strength to the weary and increases the power of the weak.
Even youths grow tired and weary, and young men stumble and fall;
but those who hope in the Lord will renew their strength.
They will soar on wings like eagles; they will run and not grow weary,
they will walk and not be faint.

Psalm 23:1-6 NIV

Thought Moment

"God uses the tension, complexity, and challenge of doing His kingdom work to transform us into champions."

Christine Caine

Week: _____

Biblical Truths _____

_____
_____
_____
_____
_____
_____
_____
_____

Reflection _____

_____
_____
_____
_____
_____
_____
_____
_____
_____
_____
_____
_____
_____
_____
_____

On my heart ♥

Gratitude

Confession

Who He is _____
_____

Prayer

_____
_____
_____
_____
_____
_____
_____
_____
_____
_____

Praise

_____
_____
_____
_____
_____
_____
_____

THINK ABOUT THESE THINGS

Finally, brothers and sisters, whatever is true, whatever is noble, whatever is right, whatever is pure, whatever is lovely, whatever is admirable—if anything is excellent or praiseworthy—think about such things. Whatever you have learned or received or heard from me, or seen in me— put it into practice. And the God of peace will be with you.

Philippians 4:8-9 NASB

Thought Moment

"You cannot have a positive life and a negative mind."

Joyce Meyer

Biblical Truths _____

_____
_____
_____
_____
_____
_____
_____

Reflection _____

_____
_____
_____
_____
_____
_____
_____
_____
_____
_____
_____
_____
_____
_____

On my heart ♥

Gratitude

Confession

Who He is _____

_____

Prayer

_____
_____
_____
_____
_____
_____
_____
_____
_____
_____

Praise

_____
_____
_____
_____
_____
_____
_____
_____
_____

LOVING OTHERS WELL

Since you have been chosen by God who has given you this new kind of life, and because of his deep love and concern for you, you should practice tenderhearted mercy and kindness to others.

Colossians 3:12 TLB

Thought Moment

"The true evidence of someone who knows they are loved is that they love well."

Lisa Bevere

Week: _____

Biblical Truths _____

_____
_____
_____
_____
_____
_____
_____

Reflection _____

_____
_____
_____
_____
_____
_____
_____
_____
_____
_____
_____
_____
_____
_____

On my heart ♥

_____
_____
_____
_____
_____
_____
_____
_____
_____
_____
_____
_____
_____
_____
_____
_____

Gratitude

_____
_____
_____
_____
_____
_____
_____
_____
_____
_____

Confession

_____
_____
_____
_____
_____
_____
_____
_____
_____
_____

Who He is _____

_____

Prayer

_____
_____
_____
_____
_____
_____
_____
_____
_____
_____
_____

Praise

_____
_____
_____
_____
_____
_____
_____
_____

THY WILL BE DONE

My [child], *do not regard lightly the discipline of the Lord,*
Nor faint when you are punished by Him;
For whom the Lord loves He disciplines,
And He *punishes every* [child] *whom He accepts.*

Hebrews 12:6 NASB

Thought Moment

"There are two kinds of people: Those who say to God, 'Thy will be done,' and those to whom God says, 'All right, then, have it your way'."

C. S. Lewis

Biblical Truths _____

_____
_____
_____
_____
_____
_____
_____
_____

Reflection _____

_____
_____
_____
_____
_____
_____
_____
_____
_____
_____
_____
_____
_____
_____
_____
_____

On my heart ♥

_____
_____
_____
_____
_____
_____
_____
_____
_____
_____
_____
_____
_____
_____
_____
_____

Gratitude

_____
_____
_____
_____
_____
_____
_____
_____
_____
_____
_____

Confession

_____
_____
_____
_____
_____
_____
_____
_____
_____
_____
_____

Who He is

_____

_____

Prayer

_____

_____

_____

_____

_____

_____

_____

_____

Praise

_____

_____

_____

_____

_____

_____

_____

HE KNOWS WE ARE DUST

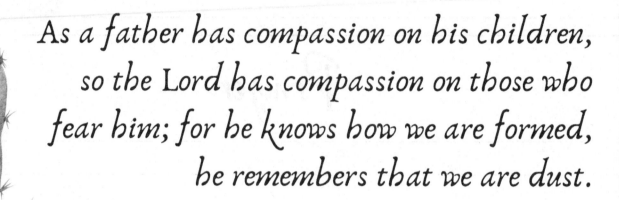

As a father has compassion on his children, so the Lord has compassion on those who fear him; for he knows how we are formed, he remembers that we are dust.

Psalm 103:13-14 NIV

Thought Moment

"The first truth we must keep in mind to overcome the lies of the pit is this: it is Satan who accuses us, not God."

Robert Morris

Biblical Truths _____

_____
_____
_____
_____
_____
_____
_____
_____

Reflection _____

_____
_____
_____
_____
_____
_____
_____
_____
_____
_____
_____
_____
_____
_____
_____
_____
_____

On my heart ♥

_____
_____
_____
_____
_____
_____
_____
_____
_____
_____
_____
_____
_____
_____
_____
_____
_____

Gratitude

_____
_____
_____
_____
_____
_____
_____
_____
_____
_____
_____
_____

Confession

_____
_____
_____
_____
_____
_____
_____
_____
_____
_____

Who He is

_____

_____

Prayer

_____
_____
_____
_____
_____
_____
_____
_____
_____
_____
_____

Praise

_____
_____
_____
_____
_____
_____
_____
_____
_____
_____

LET LOVE GUIDE YOUR LIFE

Be gentle and ready to forgive; never hold grudges. Remember, the Lord forgave you, so you must forgive others. Most of all, let love guide your life, for then the whole church will stay together in perfect harmony.

Colossians 3:13-14 TLB

Thought Moment

"An offended heart is the breeding ground of deception."

John Bevere

Week: _____

Biblical Truths _____

_____
_____
_____
_____
_____
_____
_____
_____

Reflection _____

_____
_____
_____
_____
_____
_____
_____
_____
_____
_____
_____
_____
_____
_____
_____

On my heart ♥

_____
_____
_____
_____
_____
_____
_____
_____
_____
_____
_____
_____
_____
_____
_____
_____
_____

Gratitude

_____
_____
_____
_____
_____
_____
_____
_____
_____
_____
_____

Confession

_____
_____
_____
_____
_____
_____
_____
_____
_____
_____

Who He is

_____

_____

Prayer

_____
_____
_____
_____
_____
_____
_____
_____
_____

Praise

_____
_____
_____
_____
_____
_____
_____
_____

About the Author

JOY CRABAUGH is a single mom (first and foremost!) and a dynamic business leader, but put a passion project in her hand, and it's quickly evident why her reputation as a dedicated truth-seeker and change-maker proceeds her. Through this prayer journal, she invites you on a journey of reflection and spiritual growth, allowing the truth of God, as expressed in His word, to provide a pathway to a deeper and more fulfilling prayer life.

Made in United States
Orlando, FL
28 November 2024

54602382R00124